About Demos

Who we are
Demos is the think tank for everyday democracy. We believe everyone should be able to make personal choices in their daily lives that contribute to the common good. Our aim is to put this democratic idea into practice by working with organisations in ways that make them more effective and legitimate.

What we work on
We focus on seven areas: public services; science and technology; cities and public space; people and communities; families and care; arts and culture; and global security.

Who we work with
Our partners include policy-makers, companies, public service providers and social entrepreneurs. Demos is not linked to any party but we work with politicians across political divides. Our international network – which extends across Eastern Europe, Scandinavia, Australia, Brazil, India and China – provides a global perspective and enables us to work across borders.

How we work
Demos knows the importance of learning from experience. We test and improve our ideas in practice by working with people who can make change happen. Our collaborative approach means that our partners share in the creation and ownership of new ideas.

What we offer
We analyse social and political change, which we connect to innovation and learning in organisations. We help our partners show thought leadership and respond to emerging policy challenges.

How we communicate
As an independent voice, we can create debates that lead to real change. We use the media, public events, workshops and publications to communicate our ideas. All our books can be downloaded free from the Demos website.

www.demos.co.uk

First published in 2007
© Demos
Some rights reserved – see copyright licence for details

ISBN 978 1 84180 185 8
Copy edited by Susannah Wight, London
Typeset by utimestwo, Collingtree, Northants
Printed by Iprint, Leicester

For further information and
subscription details please contact:

Demos
Magdalen House
136 Tooley Street
London SE1 2TU

telephone: 0845 458 5949
email: hello@demos.co.uk
web: www.demos.co.uk

So, What Do You Do?

A new question for policy in the creative age

Charlie Tims
Shelagh Wright

DEM⊙S

Contents

Acknowledgements

We are very grateful to Creative & Cultural Skills for supporting this work and in particular to Tom Bewick for his insight and experience, Amanda Stubbins for her ideas, support and humour, and James Evans for his research support.

In the course of producing this pamphlet we would like to acknowledge the generosity of invaluable advice, grounded creative experience and constructive criticism we received from John Newbigin, Kate Oakley, Tom Bentley, David Worthington, Lucy Newman-Cleeve, John Hartley and Stuart Cunningham of Queensland University of Technology, Charlie Leadbeater, James Purnell, Louise Wardle, Billy Grant, Indy Johal, Lise Autogena, Ellen O'Hara, Maki Suzuki, Kajsa Stahl, Jamie Stapleton and John Kieffer. They are all very passionate about this subject.

The work is largely based on several years of research with creative practitioners, creative learners and a number of intermediary agencies. There are too many people to mention but particular thanks to Creative Partnerships (especially London South and East, Kent and Durham Sunderland), Screen England, the Regional Cultural Consortia, Art Angel, East Midlands Regional Development Agency, The Last Mile, Glasgow 2020, Tate Modern, Rich Mix, Creative Kernow, Man and Eve Gallery, Engine Design, Design Heroine, Box at LSE, Arts Council England, Design Council, the Innovation Unit, Paul Roberts' Creativity Review, colleagues on the Creative Economy Programme at the Department for Culture, Media and Sport, and a number of individual artists and producers. You all know who you are and we appreciate it.

Thanks to Walter Newton for the cover illustration. At Demos, thanks to John Holden, Sam Jones, Duncan O'Leary, Pete Bradwell, Paul Miller and Catherine Fieschi for their contributions, to Laura Bunt for research support above and beyond the call of duty, and to Pete Harrington and Mark Fuller for getting this publication into print and into your hands. We hope you enjoy it even if you don't agree with it.

We are very grateful to all these and lots of other people we can't name here, but, as ever, anything we've got totally wrong or left out completely is all our own fault.

If you want to comment please get in touch.

Thanks.

Charlie Tims and Shelagh Wright
charlie.tims@demos.co.uk and shelagh.wright@demos.co.uk
June 2007

Foreword

by Tom Bewick

Dan Gerrett is a successful DJ and music producer. He is also my part-time tutor. For 12 weeks I've traded in some office hours – running the skills council for the creative and cultural industries – to make my way to a well-equipped but rather improvised studio in the back streets of east London. Two young people who have parted with over £1,000 to be on the music production course also join me. One gentleman has travelled all the way from the Midlands by coach – the cheapest form of travel – making his day, including tuition, a shattering 18-hour round trip. Not a single one of us is worried that Dan is not a real teacher – a part of an established college or training provider network. My fellow students care even less that we will not depart from his expert tutelage with an official piece of paper or a qualification to show for all the time we have put in.

That's because Dan has his own independent record label and is part of a rich and spider-like network of other music producers that span the globe. He's also an expert on the software program that for just a few hundred pounds could help spawn a lot more people like him. He embodies a new breed of 'digital' producer, every bit as powerful as the once great pioneers of Abbey Road made folklore legend by The Beatles. With vinyl obsolete and traditional CD sales in decline, people like Dan are giving established record company executives sleepless nights. According to the International Federation of Phonographic Industry (IFPI), a quarter of all music sales will be digital by 2010. Meanwhile the industry response in some quarters is to call for the drawbridge to be pulled up. This skews the public perception of the so-called 'industry' consuming precious national debate around intellectual property and copyright regulation, important as these issues are, rather than exploring new business models.

It takes a bolder person, like EMI's Eric Nicoli and his deal with Apple, for example, to be among the tentative outriders that allow for the first time high-quality downloads (at a premium) without anti-piracy protection or digital rights management software. It is a clarion call to our creative and cultural institutions everywhere – a platform on which Britain is already a global player – to resist the easy path to isolationism. Instead we should embrace the new technologies and emerging patterns of production that could make the UK the 'world's creative hub'.

It is in this new creative age where the boundary between consumer and producer is becoming increasingly blurred. With a computer laptop, keyboard and CD-burner it is now possible, in minutes, to upload an industry standard record and gain access to the coveted download and traditional charts.

There is of course a downside to this new assault on space and time, as witnessed by a lone gunman's 'multi-media manifesto', posted to US news networks just hours before the Virginia Tech massacre in April 2007. But it is also a new democratic age where among the plebeians who are blogging daily Blair and Cameron also feel the urge to get in on the act, even if they appear rather out of sorts on the MySpace and YouTube sites, which in large parts have succeeded in turning the most banal expressions of creativity into an art form.

Unlike the twentieth century, where the 'rise of meritocracy' and the notion of formal qualifications has formed a cosy consensus among the professional classes, the irreverence of the 'experience economy' prizes X-factor talent, naked ambition and who you know rather than necessarily (initially at least) what you know as more important prerequisites for success. While all these talent shows and Saturday night TV programmes may demonstrate perhaps the huge latent talent and pent-up creativity of the British people, the real creative industries hide a far shabbier secret. Forget the odd person here and there plucked from obscurity and sometimes from poverty who 'makes it' in show time. To be one of the real money-earning creative types you are far more likely to be white and male, have parents who support you financially, and live in London or the home counties. Only 4 per cent of the workforce are not white. Until 2008 there is no recognised Creative Apprenticeship route so the 'work experience, work for nothing' culture only erects further barriers to entry. The consumer appetite for creative output has never been more diverse, yet those working in these rapidly expanding industries have never been less representative of the audiences they seek to serve.

It leads to an obvious challenge to public policy discourse and whether or not it is being led in the right way. The arts community, naturally, frets at whether the Olympic preparations will squander what is widely seen as a 'golden age' for the cultural sector. The danger is that all this comes across as rather elitist – arts professionals having a conversation among themselves – rather than embracing the wider public and their priorities. There is the question of whether we really have a public support infrastructure that adds up to the greater sum of its parts. On the tenth anniversary of 'Cool Britannia' it is easy to forget what a long-term visionary Chris Smith, the first secretary of state for culture, really was, with his policy of allowing free access to museums, the public investment that allowed the Sage and the Lowry to be built, and his evidence-based approach to punching above his weight with the Treasury. All this put the creative and cultural sectors on the political and policy map. The Department for Culture Media and Sport has subsequently secured the Games in 2012, but they have also bumbled along on the Creative Economy Review Programme, taking over two years to grow the first shoots of a long awaited green paper. In 1997, such papers were churned out over a weekend. Now what should be a dynamic, creative process has turned into a Leviathan of proposed new structures and the establishment of overlapping committees.

Our current approach to publicly supporting the creative

industries or – to be more precise – creative practice isn't working. That's the stark message of this seminal report from Charlie Tims and Shelagh Wright from Demos. The valuable and informed perspectives they share are not the anodyne descriptors assigned to artistic endeavour by the hoards of these well-meaning committees set up to advise ministers. Their insights are as much a challenge to the sort of industry-led organisation that I lead as they are to government and its agencies. The authors demonstrate, however, why there is a limit on which support for the new economy can be predicated on the old ways of working. We need far greater humility to understand that non-departmental public bodies and even sector skills councils do not have all the answers. This is a post-industrial age where the kind of rigidities and perverse institutional behaviours associated with 'intervening' will not be tolerated by a consumer-savvy, techno-logically promiscuous new 'creative age' – in some instances brought up on a subversive diet of counter-cultural norms. As a number look to government to provide the answers the real solutions remain locked up in the hearts and minds of creative men and women who remain largely oblivious to the political and chattering classes talking about them.

So what's the answer? Read on.

Tom Bewick
June 2007

That question

So, what do you do? If creativity plays a big role in your life, it's probably not an easy question to answer. If you work in the creative industries, it's probably even harder. Reworking concepts, information, ideas and knowledge for a living often doesn't lend itself to a job title that adequately explains what you do. If you work in the creative industries, the chances are you work for yourself, for a small organisation or for a small team in a big organisation. You're probably working in a close network of collaborators and associates. You probably find yourself working on several different things at the same time, and many of those activities are often one-offs not to be repeated. Your job makes sense to people you work with but explaining it to people at parties becomes almost like relaying a joke that you 'really had to be there' to get.

Not being able to explain your job might be a bit awkward, but for government it's a real problem. Working in a design agency with two other people may seem a long way from government, but we rely on it to create the environments for markets to work. To date this has included creating the right tax structures, intellectual property laws and workplace legislation and, more fundamentally, fostering the right skills and capacities in people who will enter them.

Over the last ten years public policy has paid considerable attention to supporting creativity through the provision of education and skills, a copyright framework, business and innovation support, public agencies and the funding of work. But among employers, entrants and people working in the creative industries many of these interventions are resulting in confusion, indifference and, in some cases, irritation. Why? The aggregate result of jobs that are hard to understand is a sector that is hard to understand, and therefore hard to support.

Work shaped around creative projects is moving people, whether deliberately or by necessity, beyond the social and organisational categories through which work and learning have been organised in the past.

Creativity needs to be applied and supplied every day – it needs constant inputs, resources and stimuli, and thrives on reinvention. But our policy intervention assumes it can be adequately supplied through specific university courses, generic business support, a copyright framework and statutory sectoral representative bodies. The creative industries are a new way of doing business, but the policy interventions to support them proceed to work in old, industrial ways.

In this pamphlet we argue that the task for policy is no longer simply to try and pre-empt the information and knowledge that the creative industries need, but to distribute the toolkit within the sector that enables people to work it out for themselves – the means for self-production – and to find a new way to tell their collective story that adds up to the greater sum of its parts. These activities would include people working in the creative industries having improved access to:

○ *resources* digital resources for maintaining portfolios of people's learning and production life, access to potential employees and collaborators, mentors and knowledge; easy access to micro-finance, and the underwriting of risk in business loans
○ *spaces and meeting places* brokers and agencies that combine sector-specific expertise and local knowledge, that provide a point of connection to new opportunities; physical places that build networks on the model of guilds

and open members' clubs that provide a place for building informal relationships

○   *stories* a constant supply of stories provided by public agencies through competitions, research and awards that reflect back how the sector works and grows, and the value that it creates.

These are post-industrial interventions, for a post-industrial way of organising. But they are a challenge to policy-makers who tend to view the creative *industries* in standard industrial ways. Forthcoming key moments, such as the green paper on the creative economy, provide clear opportunities for policy-makers to move beyond kite-marking university courses, copyright frameworks and adapting arts policy as the key ways to support creativity.

This is a public policy challenge for the creative industries, but the question of how to be creative and sustain creative projects has massive resonance. Across the whole economy leaders are looking for new ways to unleash the creativity of their teams and organisations. In our personal lives the search for meaning and identity, the rapid pace of technological change and the collapse of traditional forms of authority give us a greater desire and need to create the world around us.

The increasing social status of creative people and the emergence of a creative class point to a new kind of inequality defined by who can and can't create, and who correspondingly is and isn't culturally visible. There are moral, market and cultural reasons for intervening to support the creative industries, but intervention will not be achieved through old ways, or with old assumptions. The challenge to support creative practice depends not on 'serving' the creative industries, but on distributing the toolkit that enables them to produce themselves. Non-stop. All day, every day.

1. Project creativity

The primary challenge of our age is how we organise ourselves for creative projects – as individuals, organisations and societies. Across the world governments are searching for the right policy environments, organisations for the right working ethos, and individuals for the right relationships that make creativity happen. Their capacity to do this will determine how well we respond to the challenges of the twenty-first century – how to tackle climate change, how to respond to aging societies, how to reinvigorate democratic societies and how to sustain the relentless need for new sources of meaning and identity.

For creativity is how we solve problems and express ourselves – a world without it is a world that doesn't exist. We rely on the products of creative organisations and creative minds to live our daily lives. From the duvet cover to the breakfast table, the toothbrush, the book you read on the bus, the keys of the computer and the organisation you work for, everything around us requires the combination of knowledge in new and original ways.

Likewise we rely on creative projects and processes to navigate our own lives, at home and at work. The disintegration of fixed long-term career paths, the decoupling of certain times of the week with certain activities, the need to manage and consume different types of media and information, the erosion of uniform family structures and social norms leave us needing to turn to creative, original solutions every day.

The era of dispersed creativity

More people have more opportunities to take part in creative projects, in more ways than ever before. If creativity relies on acquiring knowledge, synthesising, distributing and displaying it to people and finally reflecting on it, then at every stage of the process people have more tools available to aid their creativity than ever before.

knowing ➤ doing ➤ showing ➤ reflecting

This has been driven by long-term widening access to education combined with the relatively recent availability of digital and communications technologies, the falling price of material goods and the emergence of global perspectives.

Formal education

In 1970 there were approximately 130,000 people in British universities; by 2006 this had increased to 2.5 million.[1] Opportunities for formal education now stretch out over whole lives; in 2006 the Open University had 170,000 enrolled students;[2] 47 per cent of adults report that they have taken part in some form of formal education in the last three years.[3]

Cheaper, faster technology

Almost anybody who wants to access the internet in the UK can do so now. Nearly all libraries and schools are connected; 57 per cent of UK households have an internet connection, 69 per cent of which are broadband.[4] A laptop can now be bought in the UK for £600, while the advent of the '$100 laptop' may not be far away.[5] A blank tape in 1997 could hold 90 minutes of poorly recorded music. In 2007 a single DVD could hold 100 times as much. The widespread availability of shareware and open source software such as open source Java and Mozilla Firefox, and the burgeoning market for secondhand consumer electronics, have placed 'industry standard' means of production in the hands of millions.

Widening horizons

The collapse of established norms of what is and isn't good art, widening access to people, ideas and information around the world, expand the potential for the creation of new ideas, products and concepts. In 1977 the Queen's Silver Jubilee celebrations featured little more than the usual pomp and ceremony – one notable exception being a parade of 25 buses, painted silver and refurbished with carpets woven with the Queen's cipher. By 2002 the celebrations for the Queen's Golden Jubilee had expanded to include performers from countries throughout the Commonwealth, messages from children displayed in a 'rainbow of wishes', 2500 Notting Hill Carnival Performers, Hells Angels, a children's theatre group, 5000 gospel singers, floats demonstrating changes in fashion food and a pop concert featuring Brian Wilson, Paul McCartney and Baby Spice.

Markets of meaning

The rise in the capacity of so many people to make and create reflects the movement in post-industrial societies towards the continuous production and co-production of meaning as the prime determinant of economic success and human happiness. Average household spending on recreation and culture in the UK has now reached 7.9 per cent of GDP (more than any other country in the OECD).[6]

And it's everywhere – as sources of collective class-based, political, cultural and religious identity recede around us, all aspects of our life demand the production of our own forms of meaning. Creativity is sucked into the vacuum left by uncertainty.

And we see it in work, in recreation and in consumption. Visiting an Apple store is dressed as a religious experience; culture's role is recognised in international diplomacy; and across the country former industrial buildings have been fashioned into art galleries and cultural centres. In Dashanzi in Beijing, the world's biggest centre for creative and cultural industries has sprung up in former missile factories.

Creativity is motivated by the desire to create meaning. Writing a song and singing it to people. Creating a brand and people buying products imbued with it. The creative act sits somewhere between an expression of self and communication with other people. Broadly speaking there are three different 'markets' that provide opportunities for people to do this.

When we first hear the term 'markets' we tend automatically to think of exchanging money for goods – 50p for a banana, 65p for a newspaper.

The dictionary defines a market as 'an arena in which commercial dealings are conducted'. But it also refers to the original meaning of *commerce* as 'social dealings between people'.[7]

In this spirit, the markets dominated by the exchange of meaning and information are made of more than just monetary transactions. The desire to create meaning and communicate it to other people is one of the primary motivations in creative activity, and will influence the role that monetary transactions take place in it.

So, if you give someone a banana, you receive little in return. But if you sing someone a song, you might receive attention, a personal release; you might experience what Mihaly Csikszentmihalyi calls 'Flow'; and if you're lucky you might receive some applause.[8] In short, you may receive benefits other than just money.

In a 2004 survey, 90 per cent of TV and film producers in the North East say they feel 'uncomfortable' expressing their goals in commercial terms, and 18 per cent of music industry small enterprises say they are 'not about making money'.[9]

This doesn't mean that creativity is founded on altruism, or that it can only really be achieved in an absence of money, but it may mean that the 'markets' that it takes place in are made possible by more than just the exchange of money. The growth of the ways that people can be creative has fed the growth of three such 'markets' that make creativity possible: patronage, cultural consumerism and social production.

Patronage

This is one of the oldest markets for creative activity, where public and private patrons contract artists to make creative products. In the UK the biggest public patron is Arts Council England, which commissions artists and institutions on behalf of the public. On the private side, corporations sponsor artists and creatives not only to 'dress their offices', but to make works of art in their own right. Nike has recently been commissioning musicians to produce pieces of music that last approximately 45 minutes (45 minutes being the optimum time to go for a run in Nike trainers). Organisations such as Deutsche Bank, Unilever and Bloomberg all sponsor the arts. These public and private sides of commissioning are moving closer together. Public patrons look to wed people they commission to more targets and guidelines, while private patrons are looking to give artists greater freedom to grow their brands rather than just use them to soundtrack their adverts. In 2006 Becks commissioned artists to redesign its beer bottle labels. In 2007 Arts Council England commissioned contemporary artists to redesign Transport for London's Oyster-card holder.

Cultural consumerism

These markets for creativity largely emerged during the twentieth century and involve the purchase of replicable creative products produced on a mass scale, for example, the purchase of recorded music. Some of the biggest, fastest-growing markets in the world today are operating on this model; the Indian Film Industry is currently producing 1000 films a year and is growing at 19 per cent a year – it is projected to be worth $2.3 billion by the end of this year.[10] In the UK, the growing demand and the infinite shelf space of the internet have turned many of these mass markets into the niche-markets of Chris Anderson's 'Long Tail', widening the possibility for different kinds of creative activity.[11] None of the top 10 best-selling albums in the UK were released in the last ten years.[12]

Social production

An audience or a willing collaborator can provide an alternative incentive for creative production. Before the era of mass production this was how much of our culture that didn't emerge from patronage was experienced – around the piano after dinner, on the football terraces, in craft-making traditions and festivals. The internet has made it significantly easier to find and locate audiences *for* and collaborators *in* creative work. Yochai Benkler, author of *The Wealth of Networks*, calls this 'a new folk culture'.[13] These markets of 'social production' encourage creativity either because the internet provides an audience – as in the case of the blogs, Amazon reviewers, and photo-sharing sites – or because it provides willing collaborators – as in the case of open source software developers or De Montfort University's recent 'Million Penguins' attempt to write a novel via a wiki.[14] MySpace has 100 million users,[15] while 100 million videos are streamed off YouTube every day.[16]

If our culture is the 'large repertoire of solutions for the problems and passions that people consider important in each time period'[17] then it is in these three markets that people create and experience their culture. We might traditionally have thought of these areas as distinct from one another; the first market as state intervention for market failure, the second market as 'the commercial market' and the third market as anything that in the future might move into the first or second markets. But these barriers have long since receded. Rather than being distinct from one another, they form a social soup in which we learn, consume and create culture, where the roles of consumer, collaborator, competitor and client can be hard to untangle. It is from the movements between and among these 'markets' that our culture emerges and the creative industries are formed. We see this in several ways.

A young musician is likely to learn through interactions with all these markets – studying in a conservatoire, buying a new CD, checking out new music on MySpace. Likewise, when that musician grows up they will depend on these different markets to provide audiences and collaborators for their work.

Artists and producers of cultural products might be working on a public commissioned art installation one week, working on some film editing services the next and then pursuing other experiments with friends and associates.

Consumers of culture are less likely to draw distinctions between their interactions with the products of different markets. Fashion houses and designers reflect their perpetual fetish for mixing 'high and low culture', art galleries stage comedians and pop, while filmstars move between blockbusters and the West End.

Finally, the growth and visibility of the third market is feeding the supply of talent to the second market. Most musicians are now signed *after* they have become famous (on the internet) not before. But it is gradually making it easier for people, who formerly relied on a distribution industry, to enter the second market on their own terms. Taking music again, thousands of bands are able to generate revenue by playing live, as a result of distributing their music online. As a portent for things to come, Enter Shikari reached number 4 in the UK album charts on 24 March 2007 without a record deal.

These markets of meaning matter because they outline the exchanges of value that underpin economic activity and new enterprises. More importantly, they show that people are looking for a more participative role in the creation of culture and cultural expressions, rather than acting as passive recipients. As a consequence we are starting to see the emergence of a new type of inequality based on who has the skills and capacities to make and create.

Enter the creative class

The spread of creativity and creative activity is changing traditional sources of identity and status. The pointers to the elevated social status and political significance of 'creative people' operating in these markets are all around us. As the creators and arbiters of meaning, they have started to form a new elite. Richard Florida writes about the 'Creative Class' as the key to the economic success of cities.[18] The job pages are full of ads crying out for creative people. A recent GfK NOP poll of human resources directors rated 'creativity and innovation' as the most valuable asset graduates require.[19] Newspapers are full of columnists, pull-out supplements and styles that appeal to the opinion-forming creative people. Aspiring prime ministers name check The Killers for their Desert Island Discs, while identities on Facebook and MySpace heavily rely on associations with musicians and authors. The inexorable march of coffee lounges down the high street suggest that we may not all be artists or writers, but we certainly seem to want to behave more like them.

The ability to be creative has become a universal aspiration. To say that we are 'creative' suggests we hold control over the world around us – in the home, in the workplace and in the garden. Before their careers began a third of people wished that they could work in creative occupations.[20] To be creative is to prove that you have freedom in society, shows that you have economic value to employers and can fashion meaning for other people.

We are more likely to experience the products of creativity and to take part in creative processes than ever before. This has been made possible by the three markets of meaning outlined in this chapter. These have created a series of moral, economic and cultural reasons for government to be involved in supporting creative activities.

2. Politicians and pop stars

Over the last ten years the spread of creativity has filtered through into public policy-making. Human needs have economic implications. As people search for meaning, they are willing to pay for it: in the books they read, the brands they associate with, and the concerts they visit. The need to develop creative people and bring them together in creative organisations is of equal importance to our future economic prosperity and our collective well-being. Tony Blair articulated this at a speech in 2007 at Tate Modern:

> Human capital is key. The more it is developed, the better we are. Modern goods and services require high value added input. Some of it comes from technology or financial capital – both instantly transferable. Much of it comes from people – their ability to innovate, to think anew, to be creative.[21]

Governments across the world in Brazil, Denmark, India, Japan, Korea, New Zealand and Singapore have all recently been searching for ways to support creativity. Governments are looking for ways to ensure that the economy is supplied with better skills and that those skills are developed in more people.

Since the much-maligned matrimony of politics and creativity at the notorious Cool Britannia reception in 1997, an interlocking network of non-departmental public bodies, endowments, projects and initiatives has been established to support the growth of creativity in England: Creative Partnerships in schools, Culture Online to provide a 'digital bridge between culture and learning',[22] Creative & Cultural Skills in the space between education and business, and regional cultural consortia and the National Endowment for Science Technology and the Arts (Nesta) operating in support of creative entrepreneurs and innovators, to name but a few. In the regions, supported by regional development agencies, there are a host of initiatives and pilots aiming to support creativity in the economy.

But despite the emergence of a plethora of creativity-focused policies, there has been a growing scepticism that these interventions are doing their job of coherently supporting and growing creativity in the UK:

o The copyright framework for creative activity is deemed to be unfit for purpose. The Gowers Review of intellectual property recently attempted to revise it to meet the needs of a digital age.[23] The Competition and Intellectual Property Working Group of the Creative Economy Programme has suggested that copyright issues are exacerbated by weaknesses in management and business acumen in the creative industries.

o Creativity is perceived to be undervalued in education and by business. Recently the Cox Review re-examined the role of creativity in business[24] and Paul Roberts reviewed the role of creativity in statutory education.[25]

o Employers complain about the lack of creative skills in graduates. In partial response, Creative & Cultural Skills[26] has been established alongside other sector skills bodies. Creative and media diplomas and apprenticeships are being developed but take-up and access is still being tested.

o The assumptions of there being growth, business support and investment in creativity are being questioned. On one hand, the National Endowment for Science Technology and the Arts has suggested that creative industries make no special pleading to investors.[27] On the other, the Cox Review[28] suggested that creative enterprises require sector-specific support services, and the Access to Finance and the Business Support Working Group of the Creative Economy Programme suggested enterprises need to understand the priorities of private investors.[29]

o   Despite their exploitation of global culture, the creative industries remain dominated by white middle-class people (95 per cent of those working in the sector are white, while those in the key occupations are almost exclusively so), the Diversity Working Group of the Creative Economy Programme suggested a redefinition of the terms of diversity while much funding continues to drive into positive action and quota-based approaches to equality.[30]

o   Policy-making itself is not thought to be creative enough. Non-departmental public bodies have been set up to find ways of 'mainstreaming' creativity in policy-making across all departments (for example, the Innovation Unit at the Department for Education and Skills, and the Improvement and Development Agency[31] (IdEA) for Local Government).

In the dressing room at half-time

Nearly a decade on from the hype of Cool Britannia, it's half-time and creativity is back in the dressing room. After a half dominated by the manager baying different instructions from the touchline, the team has tried some new moves but is not really making the difference. The forthcoming green paper on creative industries provides a chance for a tactical rethink on creativity, but just more of the same shouting isn't going to work.

The case for public intervention in supporting creativity is sometimes unclear. The conclusion of the forthcoming green paper could appear to be obvious: stop shouting and tinkering and let the players sort it out among themselves. Who needs public intervention in the era of the kitchen-table entrepreneur? Public intervention and creativity are like pop stars and politicians – maybe the two just don't mix.

But before we dismiss the use of tactics per se, we need to ask why the ones being used are perceived to be in question. The growth of markets of meaning is making creativity more important both to realising our own individual and collective potential and the growth of economies. There is no doubt that the UK has an enviable international reputation for focusing the policy and decision-making community on the creative industries, but at home at half-time there are clearly gaps between the importance attached to creativity and the current tactics that public policy has to respond with. And this is where the football metaphor collapses. Football managers know their players inside out, but we don't understand well enough the realities of creative people and creative organisations. If we are going to understand why the tactics aren't working, we need to start with a closer examination of the people and the practices they are supporting.

3. The circus behind the industry

Creativity is produced, deployed, consumed and enjoyed quite differently in post-industrial societies from the way it used to be.[32]

A closer examination of creative people and the creative industries reveals that a gap has opened up between the micro-dynamics of creative activity in practice and the standardised interventions and responses of public policy – as a documentary-maker mentioned to us recently, 'creativity thrives on not knowing, but public policy thrives on measuring'. In shaping their work around creative projects, people are starting to push up against the social and institutional categories by which work and learning have been organised in the past. It is this tension between new ways of organising for creative activity and old assumptions that underpin interventions that cause part of our public policy response to project creativity to go awry.

Industrialising creativity

The first response to supporting creativity has been the emergence of the term 'creative industries' as a way to describe a loosely connected cluster of different types of commercialised culture.

In the UK these industries are accounted for in different ways by different agencies and departments, but broadly cover advertising, film and video, architecture, music, art and antiques markets, performing arts, computer and video games, publishing, crafts, software, design, television and radio, and designer fashion.[33] Estimates of the numbers of people working in them range from around half a million to just over one million people. In sync with other indicators of the growth in importance of creativity, they are widely thought to be growing as a sector at twice the rate of the national economy. The latest edition of the Department for Culture Media and Sport's (DCMS's) *Creative Industries Economic Estimates Statistical Bulletin* projects growth of 5 per cent in the sector.[34]

The emergence of the term creative industries and the popular discourse that has emerged around them in the UK has provided a language and a terminology that has brought the attention of many different countries towards developing their own focus on supporting the creative industries. The health of these industries is viewed as a key part of being a creative economy. In the UK, KPMG predicts 46 per cent employment growth and 136 per cent output growth in the creative industries between 1995 and 2015. In 2004 the UN estimated that creative industries account for 7 per cent of global GDP and were growing globally at a rate of 10 per cent a year.[35]

The terminology and language of the creative industries have bought a focus onto policy-making for creativity, but the term is problematic, embedding assumptions about where creativity exists and how we support it. The term implicitly assumes that the creative industries are like any other industry – like the construction industry or the nuclear power industry. But at the same time, by defining them through a human capacity – creativity – rather than by a specific product or a process for producing a product, the term also implicitly acknowledges that they are somehow different. This leaves us with an oxymoron: industries are defined by products or processes, while human capacities cannot be solely confined within industries. These ambiguities lead to different ways of accounting for and collecting data on the creative industries, and frequently recurring arguments over definitions and sub-categories. Should we count all employees within sectors? Or just the ones involved in creative activity? Some people dismiss the term wholesale, while others call for the return of the term 'cultural industries'.

Overwhelmingly, the effort to categorise, define and box creativity into an 'industry' that can be governed and regulated like any other has shrouded the eyes of policy-makers from the way that work based around creative activity and creative projects is changing people, the organisations they work for and the relationships between them.

Creative activity does not organise like a conventional industry; it organises like a flea circus.

The flea circus

However clunky the term creative industries may be, and however difficult to capture data that describes them, it is clear that in contrast to other industrial sectors, a large proportion of the players within them are small. This is a sector of huge asymmetries – a few very big players alongside a mass of micro-activity. New figures published in 2006 show us that 94 per cent of organisations in the creative industries in the UK employ fewer than ten people, 85 per cent employ fewer than five. Some 19 per cent of people working in the sector operate as freelancers.[36] Organisations employing fewer than ten people account for more than 60 per cent of employment in the sector.[37] This inclination towards a sector built around many actors shapes and results from the following rules of the organisation of this 'flea circus' of activity.

Work follows people, not organisations

The creative industries tend to be project-led, producing non-replicable outputs. As a consequence the value of the creative industries tends to be in people, and not the organisations that they work for. As John Hartley puts it, 'creativity is an input not an output . . . people apply their individual talent to the creation of something else . . . . The creative industries cannot be defined at the level of the organisation.'[38] After he recently put his architectural practice Foster and Partners up for sale, Lord Foster has been keen to emphasise his continuing involvement in the practice as his personal brand is thought to be key to the value of the company.[39]

They tend to grow by staying small

Artists don't produce endless reproductions of their own work. By the same token, people in the creative industries are motivated by the desire to create original content and respond to emerging opportunities – what Charles Landry and Franco Bianchini call 'creative deviance'.[40] This is a process that sits better in smaller organisations, less bound to the replication of the same processes and dynamic enough to create new ones quickly. This means that just as organisations grow to the size where they are visible, people tend to break off to form their own organisation, or work as freelancers, regaining their creative freedom.[41] A market trader may aspire to turn their stall into a department store, but people working in creative occupations – interested more in the meaning and money generated by their work than the size of their organisation – incline towards less grandiose designs.

They rely on personal rather than institutional trust

The creative industries emerged from the spirit of 'entrepreneurialism, individualism and doing your own thing'[42] that emerged in the 1960s. These values remain strong, resulting in a sector relying on dense networks in which people alternate between the roles of consumers, competitors and collaborators, rather than relying on big organisational systems. Contacts, knowledge and new sources of information are passed around among themselves.

Their existence is predicated on uniqueness

By its very nature the creative process involves the production of something that did not previously exist, rather than the replication of something that did. The emergence of niche markets and a service economy of increasingly specific needs demands that all organisations in the creative economy have a unique ethos, and everyone within them is able to bring unique skills. Market value is dependent on being different – making any collective terms unpopular: which of course starts with the much maligned creative industries. As John Howkins puts it:

> *The thrust of the ordinary economy is to buy as many of the same materials as possible, set up a permanent production line, and turn out as many identical products as possible . . . . In contrast, the thrust of the creative economy that deals in intangible ideas and rights, is to produce a new idea and celebrate its uniqueness.*[43]

These are the characteristics of people and organisations working in a non-stop process. Creativity doesn't need information every now and then. It needs it, every day, all of the time: how to work a new piece of software, how to find somebody to help on a project, how to find out about a new trend. Information, networks and ideas cannot be switched off. This is a flea circus of activity that never stops moving.

Organisations and individuals who are working in this way are generating the new concepts, ideas and innovations that maintain the creative industries. They may operate in small organisations or as individuals, but the rise of more flexible open-plan workspaces, flexi-time and mobile-working are indicative of the need of larger organisations to accommodate the style of the flea circus.

4. So, what do you do?

The result of the flea circus is a set of practices, ways of working and jobs that only make sense to people working in it. This is why an increasing number of people dread having to explain what they do at parties or to their relatives. What is service design or human factors analysis? What are multi-media artists and animateurs? It's easier just to make it up, isn't it?

But this has serious implications for the growth of these industries and the future of creativity. If we struggle to explain our jobs, how can we expect governments to understand how to support them? How can people thinking about working in the creative industries know what they need to do to work in them? This invisible layer of activity within the creative industries is alien to standardised industrial ways of thinking.

Knowledge flows

Gathering information about this sector and this activity will always be an imperfect exercise. Creative activity itself is a human endeavour, and will always be difficult to capture and isolate, within organisations and people. The nature of creative activity means it will often move faster than classifications, or ways of counting it. By its very nature a creative act will break one form of boundary or another. Policy can't keep up.

Governance and leadership

A sector of tiny organisations and individual unique activity is difficult to represent democratically. The loudest voices lobbying for an extension of the term of copyright for recorded music in the music industry come from the major labels, partly as there are no adequate ways of aggregating the voices of the smaller interests who have differing views. The debating groups on the future of the 'Creative Economy' set up by the DCMS in 2006 were largely drawn from representatives of publicly funded organisations. Policy is easily skewed to the visible, large and powerful.

Access and opportunity

A sector that operates in dense networks, where information, contacts and people are passed around small cliques of organisations, is a difficult one to break into. It becomes as hard for graduates to find out about the sector and the jobs they might want to enter, as it does for governments. People who access the sector are people who know people in the sector. Despite the shiny newness of the creative industries, it means they are particularly susceptible to some old ways of doing business. Opportunities favour the well connected.

Learning and doing

A sector that practises learning and doing in real time means that just as the ways of classifying them will always be trumped by their activity, so too will many preparations for working in them. It is difficult for courses and institutions to pre-empt the knowledge needs of people who will be employed in organisations who thrive on change and new opportunities; the 'feedback loops' are too short. Learning is individually defined.

A way of organising that is impossible to completely understand, govern or access and that supports and learns from itself is a huge challenge to governments. As John Hartley puts it, the creative industries 'are like perturbations on the surface of the landscape that cannot be discerned by the apparently obvious method of walking over [to] them and having a look'.[44]

It is exactly this uncertainty that creativity thrives on, but it is an uncertainty that is alien to how as a society we seek to intervene to support growth, equity and accountability. This is the source of the gap between the amorphous microdynamics of creativity in practice and the blunt instruments and standardisations of public policy and institutions, to which we will turn next.

5. I love a man in a uniform

Creativity produces highly visible outputs, but these often come from processes and people that aren't immediately visible. Take Wendy Ewald's film retelling the story of the book of Exodus in Margate.[45] The film will be screened on Channel 4, in autumn 2007, but behind it sits an enormous community arts project; a live public festival; the input of several different investors including Channel 4, Art Angel and Arts Council England; and debate in the national media and collaboration with different musicians, artists, educationalists and writers.

We began this pamphlet by looking at the visibility of creativity and creative products (like Wendy Ewald's film) in the world around us and the expansion of markets of meaning. We then went on in the previous section to look at how some of the processes that underpin creativity are difficult to make out. The result is that policy-makers tend to *recognise* the importance of creativity, but see no reason to intervene in any ways other than those they already know. This means that support for the creative industries in the UK comes either through the lens of cultural policy or as standardised support for commercial practices.

Cultural policy views the creative industries as a close relative of publicly funded arts. First, investing in cultural institutions is seen as investing in the repository of knowledge that the creative industries will draw on. Vivian Westwood recently name checked the Wallace

Collection as an inspiration for her work,[46] while Ian Brown, former singer in The Stone Roses, referenced a trip to the Natural History Museum as his inspiration for the song 'Dolphins and Monkeys'. Second, investing in publicly funded artistic practice is seen as producing the intellectual property that the creative industries can then exploit, but is unable to support itself. So for example, every year many theatre productions make it to the West End (and sometimes even Hollywood as in the case of *The History Boys* and *The Madness of King George*) after they were produced in publicly subsidised theatres and arts venues.

When not supported through 'cultural policy' the creative industries are viewed as the same as any other commercial activity. In this case policy assumes that this is a commercial sector that can be supplied with a series of inputs by public intervention. Skills for the sector come from courses. It is assumed that business advice will be the same as for any other business and that investment should be decided on the same terms as for other organisations. These interventions assume that if people in these organisations can just learn how to be better conventional managers and leaders this will result in growth in the sector evidenced in growing economies of scale. Indeed, if renegotiating copyright results in extensions over copyright terms (for example over recorded works), it will also be based on the same set of assumptions.

These two ways of supporting the creative industries have provided a blueprint for the support of the creative industries that has been echoed around the world. They have changed the ways that cities market themselves as attractive places to live. They have changed the way that cultural institutions describe their mission. And they have changed the way that universities and schools have thought about the skills they are trying to foster in learners.

But they are both fundamentally predicated on the assumption that the needs of many people in the creative industries can be wholly predicted by public policy and provided through institutions. The flea circus shows that people working with creativity need constantly to absorb information and remake it in their own way with their own communities – but those two approaches both assume that they can supply the right information at the right time in a fixed form.

These approaches translate into 'uniforms' into which people are expected to fit. While these uniforms provide a basic structure of support, and have been successful for some, they cannot fully cater for the potential and needs of people building their careers around distinct creative projects and their own creative human capital.

Uniform knowledge

People working in the creative industries need regular interaction with different groups of people to exchange ideas and know-how, and to create new responses. But investment in the infrastructure of our cultural institutions, often partly justified on the basis that they will support the creative industries, often fails to provide the effective cross-collaboration that is required. While the wider link between investment in cultural institutions and benefits for the creative industries is unclear, the existing infrastructure rarely mixes opportunities for production and consumption, with functions such as 'third' work spaces, networking and peer-learning, and exhibition/retail space.

Uniform skills

People working in the creative industries need to learn constantly in their work, not just on courses, and recruit largely through project experience and personal recommendation. But provision of training and skills is focused largely on young people, on further and higher education and on a fixed qualifications framework that bears little relation to the sector. This inevitably falls foul of two key criticisms. First, there are too many possible entrants (there are approximately 150,000 students enrolled on courses classified as Creative Arts and Design – possibly as much as 25 per cent of the entire existing creative industries workforce). Second, the quality of those with qualifications who do actually make it into the workplace do not fit the needs of employers. Some 17 per cent of creative and cultural industry businesses report skill shortages,[47] while in 2002, 21 per cent of design consultancies surveyed by the Department for Education and Skills (DfES) were 'not at all satisfied with the quality of graduates that they were receiving'.[48]

Uniform business

People working in the sector have very specific needs and are motivated by unique non-replicable acts of creativity. Work changes quickly to meet process or market opportunities, and when these opportunities occur they tend to move very quickly allowing little time for structural or skills planning. But the major provider of business support to the sector tends to apply conventional processes to this new emerging activity and may miss the specific, real-time needs and particularities of working in creative markets.

Uniform finance

Some creative activity requires dynamism and autonomy, which is easier to achieve in small organisations, but investment in the creative industries assumes that growth has to mean bigger organisations. A sector where 85 per cent of organisations employ fewer than five people is a sector that grows like an algae, not a tree. Some creative enterprises should and will remain small, which can create problems of asymmetric competition. There is evidence that although there is no absolute bias from banks and venture capitalists against investment in the creative industries, there is a scepticism about lack of tangible collateral and business planning.[49]

Uniform advocacy

People in the creative industries need a form of advocacy that reflects their working practices and needs. But advocacy for the sector rarely gets past lip service to the glossy credentials of the sector. Since the publication of Richard Florida's *The Rise of the Creative Class* (2002),[50] places around the world have scrambled to celebrate their credentials as centres for creative activity. By the same token, political leaders are keen to name check rock bands, actors and film stars in their speeches to champion the credentials of Creative Britain. But although this raised the currency of creativity, it tends to mask the everyday personal stories of people working in the creative industries, in favour of celebrity rags-to-riches stories and city branding campaigns.

The result is that government policy for creativity ends up playing bat-the-rat – struggling to hit a moving target that it can't see. It finds itself second guessing the needs of a densely networked sector, working in unique ways, feeding on new knowledge and information whose existence is predicated on reinvention. The search for how we organise government policy to support creative activity will only work if it recognises these non-stop producers.

Current assumptions unwittingly embed a different set of values into the creative process from those that motivated people in the first place. As a result, the needs of people working in the creative industries cannot be exclusively catered for by these approaches. People don't want predetermined formulae and templates to follow, but they need an alternative infrastructure through which to aggregate and exchange their production.

6. From uniforms to free forms

Creativity cannot be centrally planned – it is a self-produced activity. It emerges from the messy interactions between many different people, concepts and ideas – what Pat Kane provocatively calls 'the play ethic'.[51] Leaders of organisations have to be comfortable that they cannot know everything and that in order to respond to problems they need to foster the creativity and innovation of those they lead. The same is true for the creative industries as a sector – the role of policy is not to assume that it can fully anticipate the needs of people working in the creative industries but to distribute equitably the tools that enable people to continually self-produce all the time, every day and when they need it.

The creative industries need interventions that support non-stop production. The search for this mode of intervention is at the heart of the relationship between the citizen and the state, business and government.

Across a range of different policy areas, policy-makers are seeking to find ways of aggregating individual and small organisational activity in pursuit of various different democratic, economic and social goods.

The response to smaller organisations in the creative industries should not be to try and make them grow into larger organisations, but to develop the interventions that work with them. Rather than trying to encourage organisations to grow in order to develop economies of scale, public intervention should seek to grow economies within a sector of many small organisations.

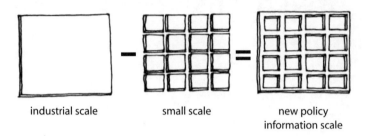

industrial scale   small scale   new policy information scale

Simply put, this is finding the tools and interventions that will fill out the space on the right-hand side of this diagram, left by a world of more individuated aspirations, preferences and organisations – what you are left with if you subtract small organisations from big organisations.

We are seeing similar efforts to produce economies of scale within a sector of many small organisations among social enterprises (organisations that work towards public goods, like charities, but within a business model).

Like people working in the creative industries, social entrepreneurs are motivated by factors other than financial remuneration. If people in the creative industries value the production of original content and meaning, then social entrepreneurs are interested in the production of public goods. This creates models of working and operation, which are outside the understanding of many of the traditional public systems of support. This is reflected in the emergence of concerted efforts to create networks and mentoring schemes between different social entrepreneurs, such as those facilitated in London in different ways by Social Enterprise London, The Hub and the School for Social Entrepreneurs.[52]

The focus for intervention that supports creativity should be the *equitable distribution of the tools of self-production and self-knowledge.* The role of public policy is not therefore to re-create a new artificial market when it fails or produces inequalities, or to try to provide standard industrial market interventions, but to stimulate our individual capacities to create new possibilities, make new connections and tell a collective story.

The toolkit for self-production

Public policy needs to develop a different kind of institutional method of co-developing resources, underpinning connections through spaces and meeting places, and telling a new story to contribute to the formation of new identities that people want to adopt and develop. The following possible responses are far from exhaustive – the toolkit will never be finished or static – but they provide some examples as a starting point to build on.

Resources . . .

. . . for creativity as a basic capacity

In the spirit of *All Our Futures*, the report published by the National Advisory Committee on Creative and Cultural Education in 1999,[53] and its reiteration in the recent Roberts Review of creativity in education,[54] the education system needs to support the development of creativity as a basic capacity in every single child. Since it was established six years ago Creative Partnerships has developed different replicable pathways to achieving this, working with creativity across the curriculum.[55] These kinds of learning opportunities should be made available as a basic entitlement for every child in England.

. . . for creative portfolios

Providing a resource for everyone from school age upwards who aspires to engage in creative projects with a web-based resource that they can use to account for their continuous creative learning and production – not just their qualifications base or the institution they attended. Public agencies could seek to develop their own portfolio platforms, or support and raise the profile of existing portfolio platforms such as the service provided by allcreativeportfolios.com. The importance of such portfolios has been repeatedly called for from *The Creative Age*[56] in 1999 to this year's Roberts Review of creativity in education.[57]

...for micro-finance

Providing small amounts of capital investment, rather than public subsidies that respond to the incremental growth patterns of individuals and organisations in the sector, providing a mixture of finance and business support. Regional development agencies could advocate or adopt the model provided by Grameen Bank in India, which enables people to secure single loans on their own terms and connects them to people who can support them. The bank now has 6.6 million borrowers. In the UK, Zopa is a 'social lending' platform that connects people directly to lenders.[58] Lenders can decide who they lend to and for what reasons. These models are predicated on the kind of trust needed in the creative industries, a small scale of activity and growth, and intimate social networks.

...for underwriting risk

Regional development agencies could act as guarantors on bank loans for operators in the creative industries, sharing risk and responsibility with entrepreneurs and private investors. The City of Austin Creative Industries Risk Underwriting Programme provides up to 50 per cent of small commercial loan risk underwritten by the city. The model provides high gearing to public investment models.[59]

Spaces and meeting places ...
...for knowledge exchange

Individuals and organisations should have access to exchange up-to-date information, lived experience and specialist knowledge of their sector. A crucial part of this would be finding a way to connect individuals with a mentor to guide them through their professional development. This activity of pairing people with knowledge and mentors could be hosted by creative brokers and hubs (as outlined below) or by supporting the role of other bodies and initiatives aiming to connect people to mentors, such as horsesmouth.com.

Creative & Cultural Skills is currently developing a Creative Knowledge Lab to provide on-demand information to help people build their knowledge of the sector and inform their choices for learning routes.

. . . for sourcing creative talent

Providing all people in the sector with a website that enables them to recruit from diverse networks of talent would widen access. This would provide a place for people to respond to and collaborate around opportunities in the sector. If integrated with portfolios it could provide a valuable resource for employers to access talent and for procurers to access skills. This could work in a similar way to Amazon's Mechanical Turk,[60] which provides a way for people to connect basic human intelligence tasks with people who are willing to do them around the world.

. . . for brokerage

New middle-men and agencies are needed that are able to support and grow networks, access opportunities, and develop partnerships based on specialised sector knowledge and local intelligence. The regional screen agencies have been developing this model over the last five years, providing expert advice to people working with moving images and making connections to local, national and international audiences.

. . . for serendipitous exchange

Investment for 'third places' (neither purely work nor social) where people can connect and grow their creative practice and social capital. These could work on the model of the old guilds, providing local meeting places, to make connections, meet colleagues, collaborators and contacts. Public agencies could form partnerships with members' clubs to create such opportunities, and galleries and museums could open up such space – the 'Club' at the Institute for Contemporary Arts being one example.

Stories ...

The flipside of distributing the toolkit of self-production is stitching together a collective story of how they are working for people – the supply of self-knowledge (so, what do *I* do?). We do not yet have a compelling story for creativity or creative industries in which the people working in them will recognise the part they play. This report has been a partial attempt to tell it. In order to inform the need for the kind of tools and interventions the creative economy needs, the sector requires a constantly re-emerging narrative. How we tell the story of the sector's protagonists and heroes, values, successes and failures influences how it grows – how university tutors think about the courses they are developing, how local policies are shaped and how we are perceived internationally. This is a crucial part of communicating Britain as the 'world's creative hub'. Public policy as storyteller should focus on creating conversation, awards, new heroes and mass.

Creating conversation

We need a policy discussion resolving how Britain communicates itself as the world's creative hub. The focus should move on from the external competition of the 'Cool Britannia' story, which emphasised that British artists and designers are innately 'more creative', to a story about our diversity, community and freedom – Britain as the hub of the world's creative activity. The emerging policy discussion around the role of culture in diplomacy and how Britain communicates itself for the Olympics are providing opportunities to start building this story.[61] The challenge is to develop this conversation further, and find practical ways of applying it.

Creating awards and new heroes

As well as celebrating their work, awards provide a positive way of telling the stories of individuals who have succeeded in a given field – they show pathways to other people. A public agency could partner a recognised brand to celebrate a particular aspect of working in the creative industries. There could be awards for kitchen table entrepreneurship, network building, the best intern/internship, the best mentor and the best loan. The American model of X Prize, which makes awards to creative ideas not yet invented, or the BAFTA 60 Seconds of Fame award to new work submitted by amateurs, also provide interesting models.

Creating mass – story storage
The web-based tools outlined in the section above could be brought together in a newsletter focusing on people weak in knowledge and networks of the creative industries – possibly school leavers, graduates, young people on internships and others entering the sector. In a similar way to the awards, this could be a partnership between a recognised brand and resources from a public agency. The newsletter could be emailed once a week, and might include personal stories of people working in the sector, requests for help, vacancies and the latest information about different sub-sectors in the creative industries. This could also create an 'archive' for the emergent sector to provide as a base for future research and development.

7. Mass creativity

In 1996 the World Commission on Culture and Development, in its report *Our Creative Diversity*, chaired by Perez de Cuellar, the former Secretary General of the United Nations, stated:

> *This truly exceptional time in history calls for exceptional solutions. The world as we know it, all the relationships we took as given, are undergoing profound rethinking and reconstruction. Imagination, innovation, vision and creativity are required. It means an open mind, an open heart, and a readiness to seek fresh definitions, reconcile old opposites and help draw new mental maps.*[62]

Ten years on, across the world, governments are still looking for the mental maps that will unleash this 'imagination, innovation, vision and creativity' in all people. The challenge in all these countries is the same: how to bridge the gap between the amorphous micro-dynamics, pace and specificities of creative activity and public policy interventions that rely on generalising the needs of people into a series of policy 'uniforms'.

Despite the UK's institutional appreciation of the importance of creativity, this is a gap that remains. We need a new series of interventions that recognise the sophistication of creative people and practices, and lead to organising and growing differently.

The interventions in this report provide a starting point for equitably putting knowledge and networks in the hands of people so that they can support themselves. When these interventions generate purchase, energy and support, they will contribute to the formation of new personal identities, growth in the capacities and capabilities of the creative industries, and the solutions to tomorrow's problems.

Recognising the complexities of supporting creative skills and organisations does not suggest that public institutions are irrelevant to their development. The imperatives for public interventions are twofold: to establish the equitable distribution of the means to be creative, and to build a coherent story of creativity through their many different real-time, purposeful connections. This is a virtuous circle – the more useful tools of public intervention are, the better public institutions will be at accumulating the knowledge that enables them to tell and reflect realistic stories about creative people and organisations. Public institutions and the creative industries will need to learn together.

The era of mass creativity is a shot in the arm for the sensory experience of freedom. The proliferation of project creativity is leading people to look for ways that they can participate and assert themselves in the production of culture and meaning. The spread of creativity is part of the evolution of our democracy and its equitable distribution is a social mission.

So, what do *you* do?

Bibliography

E Abrahamson and DH Freedman, *A Perfect Mess: The hidden benefits of disorder: how crammed closets, cluttered offices and on-the-fly planning make the world a better place* (London: Weidenfeld & Nicolson, 2006).

C Anderson, *The Long Tail* (London: Random House, 2006).

Y Benkler, *The Wealth of Networks: How social production transforms markets and freedom* (London: Yale University Press, 2006).

T Bentley, *Learning Beyond the Classroom: Education for a changing world* (London: Routledge, 1998).

D Brooks, *Bobos in Paradise: The new upper class and how they got there* (London: Simon & Schuster, 2000).

M Castells, *The Power of Identity* (Oxford: Blackwell, 2004).

M Csikszentmihalyi, *Creativity: Flow and the psychology of discovery and invention* (New York: Harper Collins, 1996).

M Csikszentmihalyi, *Good Business: Leadership, flow and the making of meaning* (London: Hodder & Stoughton, 2003).

H Davis and R Scase, *Managing Creativity: The dynamics of work and organisation* (Buckingham: Open University Press, 2000).

R Florida, *The Rise of the Creative Class* (New York: Basic Books, 2002).

TL Friedman, *The World is Flat: A brief history of the twenty-first century* (London: Allen Lane, 2005).

H Gardner, *Five Minds for the Future* (Boston, Mass: Harvard Business School, 2006).

H Gardner, *Multiple Intelligences: The theory in practice* (New York: Basic Books, 1993).

J Hartley (ed), *The Creative Industries* (Oxford: Blackwell, 2004).

J Howkins, *The Creative Economy: How people make money from ideas* (London: Penguin, 2001).

J Jacobs, *Cities and the Wealth of Nations: Principles of economic life* (Harmondsworth: Penguin, 1986).

J Jacobs, *Dark Age Ahead* (New York: Random House, 2004).

C Leadbeater, We Think: The power of mass creativity, see http://wethink.wikia.com/wiki/Main_page (accessed 25 May 2007).

L Lessig, *Free Culture: How big media uses technology and the law to lock down culture and control creativity* (New York: Penguin Press, 2004).

D Lewis and D Bridger, *The Soul of the New Consumer: What we buy and why: the quest for authenticity* (London: Nicholas Brealey, 1999).

Z Marar, *The Happiness Paradox* (London: Reaktion Books, 2003).

TJ Peters, *The Brand You 50: Or, fifty ways to transform yourself from an 'employee' into a brand that shouts distinction, commitment, and passion!* (New York: Random House, 1999).

JB Pine and JH Gilmore, *The Experience Economy: Work is theatre and every business a stage* (Boston, Mass: Harvard Business School, 1999).

D Pink, *A Whole New Mind: How to thrive in the new conceptual age* (London: Cyan, 2005).

PH Ray and SR Anderson, *The Cultural Creatives: How 50 million people are changing the world* (New York: Harmony Books, 2000).

K Robinson, *Out of Our Minds: Learning to be creative* (Oxford: Capstone Publishing, 2001).

NN Takleb, *Fooled By Randomness: The hidden role of chance in the markets and in life* (New York and London: Texere, 2001).

S Zuboff and J Maxmin, *The Support Economy: Why corporations are failing individuals and the next episode of capitalism* (London: Allen Lane, 2003).

Notes

1   Higher Education Statistics Agency, Student Tables, 'All students by institution, mode of study, level of study, gender and domicile 2005/06', www.hesa.ac.uk/holisdocs/pubinfo/student/institution0506.htm (accessed 16 May 2007).

2   Ibid.

3   NIACE, *NIACE Adult Participation in Learning Survey* (Leicester: National Institute of Adult Continuing Education, 2006), www.niace.org.uk/Research/ keyfindings/PDF/participation-survey06.pdf (accessed 16 May 2007).

4   Office for National Statistics, *Internet Connectivity: Historical monthly data*, www.statistics.gov.uk/downloads/theme_commerce/Internet_Connectivity_ back_data.xls (accessed 16 May 2007).

5   For more information on the $100 laptop foundation, see One Laptop per Child, www.laptop.org/ (accessed 16 May 2007).

6   Organisation for Economic Co-operation and Development, *OECD Factbook 2006: Economic, environmental and social statistics*, http://oberon.sourceoecd.org/vl=728798/cl=13/nw=1/rpsv/factbook/10-02-02- g01.htm (accessed 16 May 2007).

7   *Oxford English Dictionary*: 'Commerce n 1. The activity of buying and selling, especially on a large scale. 2. Social dealings between people.'

8   M Csikszentmihalyi, *Creativity: Flow and the psychology of discovery and invention* (New York: Harper Collins, 1996).

9   Nesta, *Creating Growth: How the UK can develop world-class creative businesses* (London: National Endowment for Science, Technology and the Arts, 2006), www.nesta.org.uk/assets/pdf/creating_growth_full_report.pdf (accessed 16 May 2007).

10 Indo British Partnership Network, India fact sheet, www.ibpn.co.uk/creative.asp#india (accessed 16 May 2007).

11 C Anderson, *The Long Tail* (London: Random House, 2006).

12   The Official UK Charts Company, www.theofficialcharts.com/ (accessed 16
      May 2007).
13   Y Benkler, *The Wealth of Networks: How social production transforms markets
      and freedom* (London: Yale University Press, 2006). Two fundamental facts have
      changed in the economic ecology in which industrial information enterprises
      have arisen: the basic output that has become dominant in the most advanced
      economies is human meaning and communication, and the basic physical
      capital asset to express it is the PC.
14   Million Penguins was a collaborative effort to write a novel. The project website
      used a wiki for the authors to add their submissions. For more information see
      www.amillionpenguins.com/wiki/index.php/Main_Page (accessed 16 May
      2007).
15   M Sweney, 'MySpace to tackle iTunes', *Guardian*, 4 Sept 2006,
      http://arts.guardian.co.uk/netmusic/story/0,,1864532,00.html (accessed 16 May
      2007).
16   Google Press Centre, 'Google to acquire YouTube for $1.65 billion in stock',
      press release, 9 Oct 2006, www.google.com/press/pressrel/google_youtube.html
      (accessed 16 May 2007).
17   PH Ray and SR Anderson, *The Cultural Creatives: How 50 million people are
      changing the World* (New York: Harmony Books, 2000).
18   R Florida, *The Rise of the Creative Class* (New York: Basic Books, 2002).
19   Survey quoted in D O'Leary and S Gillinson, *Working Progress* (London:
      Demos, 2005).
20   Creative & Cultural Skills, 'Creative industries score highest in dream career
      survey', press release, 3 Aug 2005, www.ccskills.org.uk/news/story.asp?pageid=
      344&siteID=1&pageTypeID=1 (accessed 16 May 2007).
21   T Blair, speech on culture at Tate Modern, 6 Mar 2007, www.number-
      10.gov.uk/output/Page11166.asp (accessed 16 May 2007).
22   C Leadbeater for DCMS, *Culture Online: The vision* (London: Department for
      Culture, Media and Sport, 2001).
23   HM Treasury, *The Gowers Review of Intellectual Property*, 2006, www.hm-
      treasury.gov.uk/media/53F/C8/pbr06_gowers_report_755.pdf (accessed 16 May
      2007).
24   HM Treasury, *The Cox Review of Creativity in Business: Building on the UK's
      strength*, 2005, www.hm-treasury.gov.uk/independent_reviews/cox_review/
      coxreview_index.cfm (accessed 16 May 2007).
25   P Roberts, *Nurturing Creativity in Young People* (London: Department of
      Culture, Media and Sport, 2006),
      www.culture.gov.uk/Reference_library/Publications/
      archive_2006/nurturing_creativity.htm (accessed 16 May 2007).
26   Creative & Cultural Skills, www.ccskills.org.uk/ (accessed 16 May 2007).
27   Nesta, *Creating Growth*.
28   Treasury, *Cox Review of Creativity in Business*.
29   DCMS, 'Access to finance and business support: final report' (London:
      Department for Culture, Media and Sport, Creative Economy Programme,

2007), www.cep.culture.gov.uk/index.cfm?fuseaction=
main.viewSection&intSectionID=339 (accessed 25 May 2007).

30   DCMS, 'Diversity: final report' (London: Department for Culture, Media and Sport, Creative Economy Programme, 2007), www.cep.culture.gov.uk/index.cfm?fuseaction=main.viewSection&intSectionID=340 (accessed 25 May 2007).

31   Improvement and Development Agency, www.idea.gov.uk/idk/core/page.do?pageId=1 (accessed 16 May 2007).

32   J Hartley (ed) *The Creative Industries* (Blackwell: Oxford, 2004).

33   The DCMS defines the creative industries as comprising advertising; architecture; the art and antique markets; crafts; design; designer fashion; film and video; interactive leisure software; music; the performing arts; publishing software and computer services; and television and radio.

34   *Creative Industries Economic Estimates Statistical Bulletin*, September 2006, www.culture.gov.uk/NR/rdonlyres/70156235-8AB8-48F9-B15B-78A326A8BFC4/0/CreativeIndustriesEconomicEstimates2006.pdf (accessed 16 May 2007).

35   Quoted in J Purnell, *Making Britain the World's Creative Hub*, speech to the Institute for Public Policy Research, 16 June 2005, www.culture.gov.uk/Reference_library/Minister_Speeches/Ministers_Speech_Archive/James_Purnell/James_Purnell_Speech01.htm (accessed 16 May 2007).

36   Creative & Cultural Skills, 'The footprint: a baseline survey of the creative and cultural sector' (London: Creative & Cultural Skills, 2006/07), www.ccskills.org.uk/media/cms/documents/powerpoint/POSTER_PP.ppt (accessed 16 May 2007). These figures include businesses in design, advertising, the arts, music and cultural heritage.

37   Ibid, table that outlines the size of organisations in the creative industries. We would recommend that in future updates of these figures, a more precise attempt is made to establish the number of people employed in organisations of fewer than ten people as a proportion of total employment in the creative industries.

38   Hartley, *Creative Industries*.

39   D Roberts and S Pfeifer, 'Lord Foster prepares to sell his practice', *Daily Telegraph*, 22 Jan 2007, www.telegraph.co.uk/money/main.jhtml?xml=/money/2007/01/21/cnfost21.xml (accessed 16 May 2007).

40   C Landry and F Bianchini, *The Creative City* (Demos: London, 1995).

41   C Leadbeater and K Oakley, *The Independents* (London: Demos, 1999).

42   A Marwick, *The Sixties* (Oxford: Oxford University Press, 1998).

43   J Howkins, *The Creative Economy: How people make money from ideas* (London: Penguin, 2001).

44   Hartley, *Creative Industries*.

45   M Bunting, 'Culture not politics is at the heart of the public realm', *Guardian*, 3 Oct 2006, www.guardian.co.uk/commentisfree/story/0,,1886128,00.html (accessed 16 May 2007).

46 V Westwood, speech at the launch of the Wallace Collection exhibition, 'Boucher: seductive visions', 29 Sep 2004.
47 Creative & Cultural Skills, 2004 Strategic Plan Skills for Creativity 2005–10,
48 DfES, *Employers Skill Survey 2002*, RR 372 (London: Department for Education and Skills, 2002), www.dfes.gov.uk/research/data/uploadfiles/RR372.pdf (accessed 16 May 2007).
49 DCMS, 'Access to finance and business support: final report'.
50 Florida, *Rise of the Creative Class*.
51 P Kane, *The Play Ethic: A manifesto for a different way of living* (London: Macmillan, 2005).
52 Social Enterprise London, www.sel.org.uk/; School for Social Entrepreneurs, www.sse.org.uk/network/index.shtml; The Hub, www.the-hub.net/ (URLs accessed 16 May 2007).
53 National Advisory Committee on Creative and Cultural Education, *All Our Futures: Creativity, culture and education* (Sudbury: Department for Education and Employment, 1999), www.culture.gov.uk/PDF/naccce.PDF (accessed 16 May 2007).
54 Roberts, *Nurturing Creativity in Young People*.
55 Creative Partnerships is an initiative based within Arts Council England that aims to broker relationships between creative practitioners and schools. For more information see www.creative-partnerships.com (accessed 16 May 2007).
56 K Seltzer and T Bentley, *The Creative Age* (London: Demos, 1999).
57 Roberts, *Nurturing Creativity in Young People*.
58 See www.zopa.com/ZopaWeb/ (accesssed 17 May 2007).
59 City of Austin, The Mayor's Taskforce on the Economy, *Austin's Economic Future, The Mayor's Taskforce on the Economy, Subcommittee Reports, 2003*, www.ci.austin.tx.us/culturalplan/downloads/mayor_taskforce_econ.pdf (accessed 16 May 2007).
60 For more information on Amazon's Mechanical Turk see www.mturk.com/mturk/welcome (accessed 16 May 2007).
61 J Holden, R Briggs and S Jones, *Cultural Diplomacy* (London: Demos, 2007).
62 World Commission on Culture and Development, *Our Creative Diversity* (Paris: Unesco, 1996), http://unesdoc.unesco.org/images/0010/001055/105586E.pdf (accessed 16 May 2007).

DEMOS – Licence to Publish

1. **Definitions**
   a **"Collective Work"** means a work, such as a periodical issue, anthology or encyclopedia, in which the Work in its entirety in unmodified form, along with a number of other contributions, constituting separate and independent works in themselves, are assembled into a collective whole. A work that constitutes a Collective Work will not be considered a Derivative Work (as defined below) for the purposes of this Licence.
   b **"Derivative Work"** means a work based upon the Work or upon the Work and other pre-existing works, such as a musical arrangement, dramatization, fictionalization, motion picture version, sound recording, art reproduction, abridgment, condensation, or any other form in which the Work may be recast, transformed, or adapted, except that a work that constitutes a Collective Work or a translation from English into another language will not be considered a Derivative Work for the purpose of this Licence.
   c **"Licensor"** means the individual or entity that offers the Work under the terms of this Licence.
   d **"Original Author"** means the individual or entity who created the Work.
   e **"Work"** means the copyrightable work of authorship offered under the terms of this Licence.
   f **"You"** means an individual or entity exercising rights under this Licence who has not previously violated the terms of this Licence with respect to the Work, or who has received express permission from DEMOS to exercise rights under this Licence despite a previous violation.
2. **Fair Use Rights.** Nothing in this licence is intended to reduce, limit, or restrict any rights arising from fair use, first sale or other limitations on the exclusive rights of the copyright owner under copyright law or other applicable laws.
3. **Licence Grant.** Subject to the terms and conditions of this Licence, Licensor hereby grants You a worldwide, royalty-free, non-exclusive, perpetual (for the duration of the applicable copyright) licence to exercise the rights in the Work as stated below:
   a to reproduce the Work, to incorporate the Work into one or more Collective Works, and to reproduce the Work as incorporated in the Collective Works;
   b to distribute copies or phonorecords of, display publicly, perform publicly, and perform publicly by means of a digital audio transmission the Work including as incorporated in Collective Works;
   The above rights may be exercised in all media and formats whether now known or hereafter devised. The above rights include the right to make such modifications as are technically necessary to exercise the rights in other media and formats. All rights not expressly granted by Licensor are hereby reserved.
4. **Restrictions.** The licence granted in Section 3 above is expressly made subject to and limited by the following restrictions:
   a You may distribute, publicly display, publicly perform, or publicly digitally perform the Work only under the terms of this Licence, and You must include a copy of, or the Uniform Resource Identifier for, this Licence with every copy or phonorecord of the Work You distribute, publicly display, publicly perform, or publicly digitally perform. You may not offer or impose any terms on the Work that alter or restrict the terms of this Licence or the recipients' exercise of the rights granted hereunder. You may not sublicense the Work. You must keep intact all notices that refer to this Licence and to the disclaimer of warranties. You may not distribute, publicly display, publicly perform, or publicly digitally perform the Work with any technological measures that control access or use of the Work in a manner inconsistent with the terms of this Licence Agreement. The above applies to the Work as incorporated in a Collective Work, but this does not require the Collective Work apart from the Work itself to be made subject to the terms of this Licence. If You create a Collective Work, upon notice from any Licencor You must, to the extent practicable, remove from the Collective Work any reference to such Licensor or the Original Author, as requested.
   b You may not exercise any of the rights granted to You in Section 3 above in any manner that is primarily intended for or directed toward commercial advantage or private monetary

compensation. The exchange of the Work for other copyrighted works by means of digital file-sharing or otherwise shall not be considered to be intended for or directed toward commercial advantage or private monetary compensation, provided there is no payment of any monetary compensation in connection with the exchange of copyrighted works.

    c   If you distribute, publicly display, publicly perform, or publicly digitally perform the Work or any Collective Works, You must keep intact all copyright notices for the Work and give the Original Author credit reasonable to the medium or means You are utilizing by conveying the name (or pseudonym if applicable) of the Original Author if supplied; the title of the Work if supplied. Such credit may be implemented in any reasonable manner; provided, however, that in the case of a Collective Work, at a minimum such credit will appear where any other comparable authorship credit appears and in a manner at least as prominent as such other comparable authorship credit.

5. **Representations, Warranties and Disclaimer**

    a   By offering the Work for public release under this Licence, Licensor represents and warrants that, to the best of Licensor's knowledge after reasonable inquiry:

        i   Licensor has secured all rights in the Work necessary to grant the licence rights hereunder and to permit the lawful exercise of the rights granted hereunder without You having any obligation to pay any royalties, compulsory licence fees, residuals or any other payments;

        ii The Work does not infringe the copyright, trademark, publicity rights, common law rights or any other right of any third party or constitute defamation, invasion of privacy or other tortious injury to any third party.

    b   EXCEPT AS EXPRESSLY STATED IN THIS LICENCE OR OTHERWISE AGREED IN WRITING OR REQUIRED BY APPLICABLE LAW, THE WORK IS LICENCED ON AN "AS IS" BASIS, WITHOUT WARRANTIES OF ANY KIND, EITHER EXPRESS OR IMPLIED INCLUDING, WITHOUT LIMITATION, ANY WARRANTIES REGARDING THE CONTENTS OR ACCURACY OF THE WORK.

6. **Limitation on Liability.** EXCEPT TO THE EXTENT REQUIRED BY APPLICABLE LAW, AND EXCEPT FOR DAMAGES ARISING FROM LIABILITY TO A THIRD PARTY RESULTING FROM BREACH OF THE WARRANTIES IN SECTION 5, IN NO EVENT WILL LICENSOR BE LIABLE TO YOU ON ANY LEGAL THEORY FOR ANY SPECIAL, INCIDENTAL, CONSEQUENTIAL, PUNITIVE OR EXEMPLARY DAMAGES ARISING OUT OF THIS LICENCE OR THE USE OF THE WORK, EVEN IF LICENSOR HAS BEEN ADVISED OF THE POSSIBILITY OF SUCH DAMAGES.

7. **Termination**

    a   This Licence and the rights granted hereunder will terminate automatically upon any breach by You of the terms of this Licence. Individuals or entities who have received Collective Works from You under this Licence, however, will not have their licences terminated provided such individuals or entities remain in full compliance with those licences. Sections 1, 2, 5, 6, 7, and 8 will survive any termination of this Licence.

    b   Subject to the above terms and conditions, the licence granted here is perpetual (for the duration of the applicable copyright in the Work). Notwithstanding the above, Licensor reserves the right to release the Work under different licence terms or to stop distributing the Work at any time; provided, however that any such election will not serve to withdraw this Licence (or any other licence that has been, or is required to be, granted under the terms of this Licence), and this Licence will continue in full force and effect unless terminated as stated above.

8. **Miscellaneous**

    a   Each time You distribute or publicly digitally perform the Work or a Collective Work, DEMOS offers to the recipient a licence to the Work on the same terms and conditions as the licence granted to You under this Licence.

    b   If any provision of this Licence is invalid or unenforceable under applicable law, it shall not affect the validity or enforceability of the remainder of the terms of this Licence, and without further action by the parties to this agreement, such provision shall be reformed to the minimum extent necessary to make such provision valid and enforceable.

    c   No term or provision of this Licence shall be deemed waived and no breach consented to unless such waiver or consent shall be in writing and signed by the party to be charged with such waiver or consent.

    d   This Licence constitutes the entire agreement between the parties with respect to the Work licensed here. There are no understandings, agreements or representations with respect to the Work not specified here. Licensor shall not be bound by any additional provisions that may appear in any communication from You. This Licence may not be modified without the mutual written agreement of DEMOS and You.